D1058700

100
INSPIRATIONAL QUOTES
BY *JOYCE MEYER*

AND THE LIFE-CHANGING SCRIPTURES BEHIND THEM

Throughout the 40 plus years that I've been privileged to teach God's Word, He has given me ways to communicate biblical principles so that they really strike a chord with people. It's so exciting when this happens because my life's goal is to help people understand the Bible and learn how to apply it to their lives, and my prayer is this book will help you do just that!

As you read it, you'll find brief points God has given me in my teachings that you can easily take in and think about as you go through your day. Each quote has an accompanying Scripture verse (or verses) that gives the biblical truth behind it. This is important because it's the Truth God gives us that makes a life-changing difference — not the thoughts or opinions of another person.

My hope is that you will use this resource to help keep your mind focused on God and His Word; it could also be a starting point for a Bible study. Maybe you not only need a brief word of encouragement, but some direction to go deeper in what God has to say about a challenging situation you're facing. You can take the key scripture listed with the quote that inspires you and do key word studies of terms in the verse or look up other verses that speak to the topic in a concordance. I also want to encourage you to pray as you meditate on the Word, asking the Holy Spirit to teach you what you need to know. He is THE Teacher, as John 14:26 tells us.

Keep God first in everything you do and every part of your life. He loves you and always has your best interest at heart. Trust Him to guide you through His Word in your everyday life, and you'll enjoy your journey!

Joyce

"For as he thinks in his heart, so is he...."
- **PROVERBS 23:7 NKJV**

Where the mind goes,
the man follows.

"Do not conform to the pattern of this world, but be transformed by the renewing of your mind. Then you will be able to test and approve what God's will is—his good, pleasing and perfect will."

ROMANS 12:2 NIV

You can change your life by letting the Word of God change your mind.

God doesn't just give you the dream; He gifts you the faith to believe it!

"Now faith is the assurance (the confir-mation, the title deed) of the things [we] hope for, being the proof of things [we] do not see and the conviction of their reality [faith perceiving as real fact what is not revealed to the senses]."

HEBREWS 11:1 AMPC

"For a day in Your courts is better than a thousand [anywhere else]; I would rather stand [as a door-keeper] at the threshold of the house of my God than to live [at ease] in the tents of wickedness."

PSALM 84:10

In your journey

with Jesus, your worst day with Him will always be better than your best day without Him.

I may not be w
but thank God
used to be. I'm
my way!

re I need to be,
n not where I
ay and I'm on

"And we all...continually seeing as in a mirror the glory of the Lord, are progressively being transformed into His image from [one degree of] glory to [even more] glory, which comes from the Lord, [who is] the Spirit." **2 CORINTHIANS 3:18**

"This is how God showed his love among us: He sent his one and only Son into the world that we might live through him. This is love: not that we loved God, but that he loved us and sent his Son as an atoning sacrifice for our sins."

1 JOHN 4:9-10 NIV

I don't need to *do* something important to be important; I am important because God loves me and He sent Jesus to die for me.

God can do more for you in a minute than you can do in a lifetime.

"Now all glory to God, who is able, through his mighty power at work within us, to accomplish infinitely more than we might ask or think."

EPHESIANS 3:20 NLT

We get into trouble when we start expecting people to do for us what only God can do.

"'The Lord is my portion,' says my soul,
'Therefore I hope in Him!'"

God created us to please Him, which sets us free from the need to please people. Be a God-pleaser, not a people-pleaser.

"Am I now trying to win the favor and approval of men, or of God? Or am I seeking to please someone? If I were still trying to be popular with men, I would not be a bond servant of Christ." **—GALATIANS 1:10**

"Let us then approach God's throne of grace with confidence, so that we may receive mercy and find grace to help us in our time of need."

HEBREWS 4:16 NIV

Always go to God first when you have a problem. Go to the throne, not the phone.

Stop trying to give God everything you are and start giving Him everything you are not. His strength is made perfect in our weakness!

"And He said to me, 'My grace is sufficient for you, for My strength is made perfect in weakness.' Therefore most gladly I will rather boast in my infirmities, that the power of Christ may rest upon me."

2 CORINTHIANS 12:9 NKJV

Remember

God is not surprised by your faults. He knew about them before you did, and He loves you anyway!

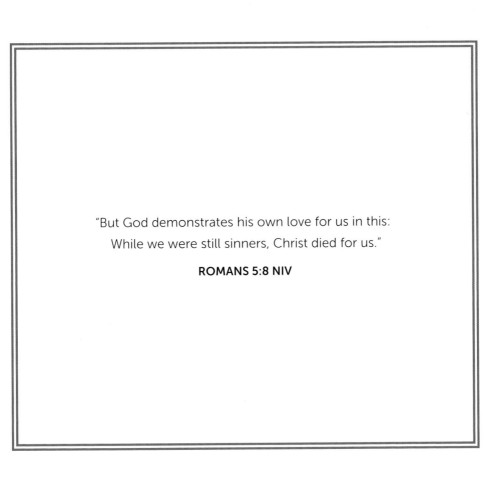

"But God demonstrates his own love for us in this:
While we were still sinners, Christ died for us."

ROMANS 5:8 NIV

We don't need
we need God-c

lf-confidence;
fidence.

"Everything else is worthless when compared with the infinite value of knowing Christ Jesus my Lord. For his sake I have discarded everything else, counting it all as garbage, so that I could gain Christ and become one with him. I no longer count on my own righteousness through obeying the law; rather, I become righteous through faith in Christ...."

PHILIPPIANS 3:8-9 NLT

New level, new devil!

"For a wide door of opportunity for effectual [service] has opened to me [there, a great and promising one], and [there are] many adversaries."

1 CORINTHIANS 16:9 AMPC

We need to take God out of our "emergency only" box and allow Him into our everyday life.

"Trust in and rely
confidently on the
Lord with all your
heart and do not rely
on your own insight
or understanding. In
all your ways know
and acknowledge and
recognize Him, and
He will make your
paths straight and
smooth...."

PROVERBS 3:5-6

"Get wisdom,
get understanding;
do not forget my
words or turn away
from them. Do not
forsake wisdom, and
she will protect you;
love her, and she will
watch over you."

PROVERBS 4:5-6 NIV

Wisdom
you wil
Be c
yourse
matter how
or what

ans doing now what

e happy with later on.

rmined to discipline

do what's right – no

i feel, what you think

erybody else is doing.

"Now every athlete who [goes into training and] competes in the games is disciplined and exercises self-control in all things. They do it to win a crown that withers, but we [do it to receive] an imperishable [crown that cannot wither]."

—1 CORINTHIANS 9:25

You can't have authority over the devil if you can't get authority over a sink full of dirty dishes.

You can feel "wrong" and still do what's right. Start choosing to do what you know is right and eventually your feelings will catch up.

"Do not let sin control the way you live; do not give in to sinful desires. Do not let any part of your body become an instrument of evil to serve sin. Instead, give yourselves completely to God, for you were dead, but now you have new life. So use your whole body as an instrument to do what is right for the glory of God."

ROMANS 6:12-13 NLT

39

Don't mourn
bad decisions;
overcome them
with good ones.

"I call heaven and earth as
witnesses against you today, that
I have set before you life and death, the
blessing and the curse; therefore, you
shall choose life in order that you may
live, you and your descendants."

DEUTERONOMY 30:19

"But you, O Lord, are a God of compassion and mercy, slow to get angry and filled with unfailing love and faithfulness."

PSALM 86:15 NLT

There is

never one
moment

in your life when God doesn't
love you!

Expect som
to happen t

hing good
ou today!

"Therefore the Lord waits [expectantly] and longs to be gracious to you, and therefore He waits on high to have compassion on you. For the Lord is a God of justice; blessed (happy, fortunate) are all those who long for Him [since He will never fail them]." ISAIAH 30:18

"For if you are trying to make yourselves right with God by keeping the law, you have been cut off from Christ! You have fallen away from God's grace. But we who live by the Spirit eagerly wait to receive by faith the righteousness God has promised to us. For when we place our faith in Christ Jesus, there is no benefit in being circumcised or being uncircumcised. What is important is faith expressing itself in love."

GALATIANS 5:4-6 NLT

Do good works *because* **you love God,** not to get **Him** to love you.

Always value your reputation with God more than your reputation with man.

"For we speak as messengers approved by God to be entrusted with the Good News. Our purpose is to please God, not people. He alone examines the motives of our hearts."

1 THESSALONIANS 2:4 NLT

"...He Who lives in you is greater (mightier) than he who is in the world."

1 JOHN 4:4 AMPC

My attitude
belongs to me and
I can decide what
it is going to be.

Stop wishing and start
pressing. We don't need
more wishbone,
we need backbone!

"Finally, be strong in the Lord and in his mighty power. Put on the full armor of God, so that you can take your stand against the devil's schemes. For our struggle is not against flesh and blood, but against rulers, against the authorities, against the powers of this dark world and against the spiritual forces of evil in the heavenly realms."

—**EPHESIANS 6:10-12 NIV**

"I know that there is nothing better for people than to be happy and to do good while they live. That each of them may eat and drink, and find satisfaction in all their toil— this is the gift of God."

ECCLESIASTES 3:12-13 NIV

Embrace the season of life you are in and squeeze all the joy out of it that you can.

If we talk to God in the morning before we talk to anyone else, we will be a lot easier to get along with.

"Listen to my voice in the morning, Lord. Each morning I bring my requests to you and wait expectantly."

PSALM 5:3 NLT

Through God's grace.

we can live upright
instead of *uptight*.

"[All] are justified and made upright and in right standing with God, freely and gratuitously by His grace (His unmerited favor and mercy), through the redemption which is [provided] in Christ Jesus."

ROMANS 3:24 AMPC

Think beautif
there will be
ugly ones.

thoughts and room for the

"Those who live according to the flesh have their minds set on what the flesh desires; but those who live in accordance with the Spirit have their minds set on what the Spirit desires." **ROMANS 8:5 NIV**

Sometimes God
uses the junk in other
people to pull the
junk out of you.

"Iron sharpens iron; so a man sharpens the countenance of his friend [to show rage or worthy purpose]."

PROVERBS 27:17 AMPC

We only have one life to give and we should be careful who and what we give it to.

"Whatever you do [whatever your task may be], work from the soul [that is, put in your very best effort], as [something done] for the Lord and not for men."

COLOSSIANS 3:23

"You, my brothers and sisters, were called to be free. But do not use your freedom to indulge the flesh; rather, serve one another humbly in love."

GALATIANS 5:13 NIV

True freedom is not getting everything you want; it's being able to be happy and emotionally stable when you don't get what you want.

"But love [that is, unselfishly seek the best or higher good for] your enemies, and do good, and lend, expecting nothing in return; for your reward will be great (rich, abundant), and you will be sons of the Most High...."

—**LUKE 6:35**

Forgive your enemies quickly.
Your anger won't change them,
so why be miserable all day?
God is your Vindicator!

"For You formed my inner-most parts; You knit me [together] in my mother's womb. I will give thanks and praise to You, for I am fearfully and wonderfully made; wonderful are Your works, and my soul knows it very well."

PSALM 139:13-14

We are human beings, not human doings.

To delight yourself in the Lord and let Him give you the desires of your heart is much better than struggling while trying to get things for yourself.

"Delight yourself also in the Lord,
and He will give you the desires
and secret petitions of your heart."

PSALM 37:4 AMPC

"Let the peace of Christ [the inner calm of one who walks daily with Him] be the controlling factor in your hearts [deciding and settling questions that arise]. To this peace indeed you were called as members in one body [of believers]. And be thankful [to God always]."

COLOSSIANS 3:15

What truly matters

in life is what's happening IN us, not what's happening around us.

You are most li[kely]
you are good t[o]
deserve it.

God when
hose who don't

"You have heard that is was said, You shall love your neighbor and hate your enemy; but I tell you, Love your enemies and pray for those who persecute you, to show that you are the children of your Father Who is in heaven...." **MATTHEW 5:43-45 AMPC**

"Then they asked Him, 'What are we to do, so that we may habitually be doing the works of God?' Jesus answered, 'This is the work of God: that you believe [adhere to, trust in, rely on, and have faith] in the One whom He has sent.'"

JOHN 6:28-29

Fear is a dead end but faith always has a future!

Gratitude is a great energizer. The more thankful you are, the better you will feel!

"I will sing of your strength, in the morning I will sing of your love; for you are my fortress, my refuge in times of trouble. You are my strength, I sing praise to you; you, God, are my fortress, my God on whom I can rely."

PSALM 59:16-17 NIV

"You were taught, with regard to your former way of life, to put off your old self, which is being corrupted by its deceitful desires; to be made new in the attitude of your minds; and to put on the new self, created to be like God in true righteousness and holiness."

EPHESIANS 4:22-24 NIV

It isn't what other people think of us that hurts us—it's what we think of ourselves.

There's nothing better than peace. Peace equals more power in your life!

"May the God of your hope so fill you with all joy and peace in believing [through the experience of your faith] that by the power of the Holy Spirit you may abound and be overflowing (bubbling over) with hope." —ROMANS 15:13 AMPC

"You are the salt
of the earth...."

MATTHEW 5:13

Our lives are meant to be salty. They should make others thirsty for God.

Pray first and then make plans. Don't plan and then pray for your plan to work.

"Be persistent and devoted to prayer,
being alert and focused in your prayer
life with an attitude of thanksgiving."

COLOSSIANS 4:2

One of the

best
statements

you can ever make in
your relationships is:

*"I think I'm right
but I may be wrong."*

"If possible, as far as it depends on you,
live at peace with everyone."

ROMANS 12:18

God never ask **anything with** **ability to do it**

us to do
t giving us the

"I can do all things [which He has called me to do] through Him who strengthens and empowers me [to fulfill His purpose—I am self-sufficient in Christ's sufficiency; I am ready for anything and equal to anything through Him who infuses me with inner strength and confident peace.]" **PHILIPPIANS 4:13**

It's okay to enjoy your life while you have a problem. Being miserable won't make it go away any faster.

"Who of you by worrying can add one hour to [the length of] his life?"

MATTHEW 6:27

95

You can be at peace with your past, content with your present, and sure about your future, knowing that God loves you!

"For I know the thoughts and plans that I have for you, says the Lord, thoughts and plans for welfare and peace and not for evil, to give you hope in your final outcome."

JEREMIAH 29:11 AMPC

"Do nothing from selfishness or empty conceit [through factional motives, or strife], but with [an attitude of] humility [being neither arrogant nor self-righteous], regard others as more important than yourselves."

PHILIPPIANS 2:3

The less self-focused we are, the happier we are going to be. It is not possible to be happy and selfish at the same time.

"When You said, 'Seek My face [in prayer, require My presence as your greatest need],' my heart said to You, 'Your face, O Lord, I will seek [on the authority of Your word].'" —**PSALM 27:8**

Seek God's face, not His hand – who He is, not just what He can do for you.

"I have been crucified with Christ and I no longer live, but Christ lives in me. The life I now live in the body, I live by faith in the Son of God, who loved me and gave himself for me."

GALATIANS 2:20 NIV

What God gives
me by His grace
is His gift to me.
How I live my life
is my gift to God.

You can't keep doing
thing over and over
you're going to get a
Let's learn to maxin
by maximizing our

same
think
ter result.
our lives
e.

"To everything there
is a season, and a time
for every matter or
purpose under heaven."

ECCLESIASTES 3:1 AMPC

"Do not be overcome and conquered by evil,
but overcome evil with good."

ROMANS 12:21

Don't waste another day
of your life being angry.
You can forgive

on purpose.

love on purpose and give on
purpose. So get happy
and do good!

We have to get o
everything shou
Get rid of the sta
too hard!" Beca
leads us to do is

r thinking
be easy for us.
ment "It's just
e nothing God
o hard.

"For it is [not your strength, but it is] God who is effectively at work in you, both to will and to work [that is, strengthening, energizing, and creating in you the longing and the ability to fulfill your purpose] for His good pleasure." **PHILIPPIANS 2:13**

"...Clothe yourselves with humility toward one another [tie on the servant's apron], for God is opposed to the proud [the disdainful, the presumptuous, and He defeats them], but He gives grace to the humble. Therefore humble yourselves under the mighty hand of God [set aside self-righteous pride], so that He may exalt you [to a place of honor in His service] at the appropriate time."

1 PETER 5:5-6

You can be pitiful or powerful, but you can't be both. Give up the self-pity and get on with life!

We can't control
what other people
do and how they
decide to treat us,
but we can control
our response to them.

"Get rid of all bit-
terness, rage and
anger, brawling and
slander, along with
every form of malice.
Be kind and compas-
sionate to one an-
other, forgiving each
other, just as in Christ
God forgave you."

EPHESIANS 4:31-32 NIV

113

"...In love He predestined and lovingly planned for us to be adopted to Himself as [His own] children through Jesus Christ, in accordance with the kind intention and good pleasure of His will."

EPHESIANS 1:4-5

Jesus did not die to give us a religion. He died so that through faith in Him, we could have an intimate relationship with God.

No matter what you have gone through or might be going through right now, you can hope (have faith) that God is working on your behalf right now, and you will see the results of His work in your life. You don't have to be a prisoner of your circumstances, but instead you can be a prisoner of hope!

"Return to the stronghold [of security and prosperity], O prisoners who have the hope; even today I am declaring that I will restore double [your former prosperity] to you...."

—ZECHARIAH 9:12

"Let there be no filthiness and silly talk, or coarse [obscene or vulgar] joking, because such things are not appropriate [for believers]; but instead speak of your thankfulness [to God]."

EPHESIANS 5:4

Complaining keeps us from seeing the blessings we do have. Gratitude is the antidote for the poison of complaining.

I know that I know that the Word of God works, and if you will really believe it, you will be completely transformed. It is full of power to bring healing to every area of your life!

"All Scripture is inspired by God and is useful to teach us what is true and to make us realize what is wrong in our lives. It corrects us when we are wrong and teaches us to do what is right. God uses it to prepare and equip his people to do every good work."

2 TIMOTHY 3:16-17 NLT

God is a giver, and when we **give unselfishly.** we are more like Him than at any other time in our lives.

"A new command I give you: Love one another.
As I have loved you, so you must love one another."

JOHN 13:34 NIV

Indifference m
but love finds
refuse to do no

es an excuse,
vay; therefore, I
ing!

"Righteousness and justice are the foundation
of Your throne; mercy and loving-kindness and
truth go before Your face." **PSALM 89:14 AMPC**

Jesus died for us to have abundant life. That doesn't mean we won't have any problems; it means there's a place in God where we can live above the problems of life.

"These things I have spoken to you, that in Me you may have peace. In the world you will have tribulation; but be of good cheer, I have overcome the world."

JOHN 16:33 NKJV

Jesus came to heal the brokenhearted and set the captives free. He can heal you EVERYWHERE you hurt!

"The Spirit of the Lord God is upon me, because the Lord has anointed and commissioned me to bring good news to the humble and afflicted; He has sent me to bind up [the wounds of] the brokenhearted, to proclaim release [from confinement and condemnation] to the [physical and spiritual] captives and freedom to prisoners."

ISAIAH 61:1

"...We also glory in our sufferings, because we know that suffering produces perseverance; perseverance, character; and character, hope. And hope does not put us to shame, because God's love has been poured out into our hearts through the Holy Spirit, who has been given to us."

ROMANS 5:3-5 NIV

Maybe where you are right now is not your fault, but don't let what happened to you become an excuse to stay that way.

"I am the Vine; you are the branches. The one who remains in Me and I in him bears much fruit, for [otherwise] apart from Me [that is, cut off from vital union with Me] you can do nothing." —**JOHN 15:5**

I'm an everything-nothing: I'm everything with Jesus and nothing without Him!

"Death and life are in the power of the tongue, and those who love it and indulge it will eat its fruit and bear the consequences of their words."

PROVERBS 18:21

Words are
containers for
power. The power
of life and death
is in the tongue.

We need to make the decision to enjoy every single day of our lives. It's not irresponsible to enjoy your life while you have a problem.

"Give all your worries and cares to God,
for he cares about you."

1 PETER 5:7 NLT

"But He gives us more and more grace [through the power of the Holy Spirit to defy sin and live an obedient life that reflects both our faith and our gratitude for our salvation]...."

JAMES 4:6

Grace

is not an excuse to live a sloppy life and get by with it; it's the power not to have to live a sinful life.

Prayer is the gre
have. It's not a du
last-ditch effort; i
our first line of d

est privilege we
obligation or
hould always be
ense.

"Be unceasing in prayer [praying perseveringly]." **1 THESSALONIANS 5:17 AMPC**

"...Every healthy tree bears good fruit, but the unhealthy tree bears bad fruit. A good tree cannot bear bad fruit, nor can a bad tree bear good fruit."

MATTHEW 7:17-18

There's a difference between being busy and being fruitful. Are you busy or fruitful?

When you really know who God is – that He's for you and not against you, that He loves you, that He's the source of everything you need – then life gets really exciting!

"For from Him [all things originate] and through Him [all things live and exist] and to Him are all things [directed]. To Him be glory and honor forever! Amen."

ROMANS 11:36

"For this reason I am telling you, whatever things you ask for in prayer [in accordance with God's will], believe [with confident trust] that you have received them, and they will be given to you."

MARK 11:24

We get what we believe for. I'd rather believe for a lot and get half of it than believe for nothing and get all of it.

Take time to deal with little problems and you won't have to spend more time dealing with big ones.

"Look carefully then how you walk! Live purposefully and worthily and accurately, not as the unwise and witless, but as wise (sensible, intelligent people)."

—**EPHESIANS 5:15 AMPC**

"A calm and undisturbed mind and heart are the life and health of the body, but envy, jealousy, and wrath are like rottenness of the bones."

PROVERBS 14:30 AMPC

Your ability to defeat stress is determined by what's going on *inside* of you, not by what's going on outside of you in your circumstances.

It's what we do right consistently—over and over—that changes us.

"My son, do not let wisdom and understanding out of your sight, preserve sound judgment and discretion; they will be life for you, an ornament to grace your neck. Then you will go on your way in safety, and your foot will not stumble."

PROVERBS 3:21-23 NIV

God can

completely restore us

no matter what
we've done or been through.
He wants to give us
double for our trouble!

"Instead of your [former] shame you will have a double portion; and instead of humiliation your people will shout for joy over their portion. Therefore in their land they will possess double [what they had forfeited]; everlasting joy will be theirs."

ISAIAH 61:7

There is an an
problem in th
The Bible is ou
book for life!

ver for every
Word of God.
nstruction

"Your word is a lamp to my feet and a light to my path." **PSALM 119:105**

There is no worse life than always being wrapped up in yourself with a "What about me?!" mentality.

"And He died for all, so that all those who live might live no longer to and for themselves, but to and for Him Who died and was raised again for their sake."

2 CORINTHIANS 5:15 AMPC

Contrary to popular opinion, you don't always have to give your feelings a vote. Learn how to live beyond your feelings!

"For if you are living according to the [impulses of the] flesh, you are going to die. But if [you are living] by the [power of the Holy] Spirit you are habitually putting to death the sinful deeds of the body, you will [really] live forever."

ROMANS 8:13

"Study and be eager and do your utmost to present yourself to God approved (tested by trial), a workman who has no cause to be ashamed, correctly analyzing and accurately dividing [rightly handling and skillfully teaching] the Word of Truth."

2 TIMOTHY 2:15 AMPC

The hard thing is hard for a reason: it yields the greatest reward. You can't have the perks without the work!

"...God is light; in him there is no darkness at all. If we claim to have fellowship with him and yet walk in darkness, we lie and do not live out the truth. But if we walk in the light, as he is in the light, we have fellowship with one another, and the blood of Jesus, his Son, purifies us from all sin."   —1 JOHN 1:5-7 NIV

Right behavior never produces a right relationship with God, but a right relationship with God will ALWAYS produce right behavior.

"...Jesus said, 'If you hold to my teaching, you are really my disciples. Then you will know the truth, and the truth will set you free.'"

JOHN 8:31-32 NIV

Our secrets make us sick but God's truth sets us free!

Learn how to live in agreement, even if it means you disagree agreeably.

"Don't have anything to do with foolish and stupid arguments, because you know they produce quarrels. And the Lord's servant must not be quarrelsome but must be kind to everyone, able to teach, not resentful."

2 TIMOTHY 2:23-24 NIV

"Now no chastening seems to be joyful for the
present, but painful; nevertheless, afterward
it yields the peaceable fruit of righteousness
to those who have been trained by it."

HEBREWS 12:11 NKJV

I love the school of the

Holy Spirit

because you never flunk out.
You just keep taking the test
over and over until you pass.

Love is not som it's who He is.

hing God does–

"The one who does not love has not become acquainted with God [does not and never did know Him], for God is love. [He is the originator of love, and it is an enduring attribute of His nature.]" **1 JOHN 4:8**

"...For the one who wavers (hesitates, doubts) is like the billowing surge out at sea that is blown hither and thither and tossed by the wind. For truly, let not such a person imagine that he will receive anything [he asks for] from the Lord."

JAMES 1:6-7 AMPC

We have to learn how to doubt our doubts and make a determined decision to trust God no matter how we feel, what we think or what the circumstance looks like.

There's no such thing as a drive-through breakthrough, and there's no such thing as microwave maturity.

"Remain in Me, and I [will remain] in you. Just as no branch can bear fruit by itself without remaining in the vine, neither can you [bear fruit, producing evidence of your faith] unless you remain in Me."

JOHN 15:4

"Blessed [happy, spiritually prosperous, favored by God] is the man who is steadfast under trial and perseveres when tempted; for when he has passed the test and been approved, he will receive the [victor's] crown of life which the Lord has promised to those who love Him."

JAMES 1:12

Everyone wants to be an overcomer but nobody wants to have anything to overcome. You can't have a testimony without a test!

We're not really free until
we're free from the need
to impress other people.

"In your relationships with one another, have the same mindset as Christ Jesus: Who, being in very nature God, did not consider equality with God something to be used to his own advantage; rather, he made himself nothing by taking the very nature of a servant, being made in human likeness." —**PHILIPPIANS 2:5-7 NIV**

"And Abraham's faith did not weaken, even though, at about 100 years of age, he figured his body was as good as dead—and so was Sarah's womb. Abraham never wavered in believing God's promise. In fact, his faith grew stronger, and in this he brought glory to God. He was fully convinced that God is able to do whatever he promises."

ROMANS 4:19-21 NLT

Faith always requires unanswered questions. If we knew everything we want to know all the time, we wouldn't need faith to get us through things.

We serve a God
of more than
enough, not
barely enough.

"And my God will liberally supply
(fill until full) your every need according
to His riches in glory in Christ Jesus."

PHILIPPIANS 4:19

Don't get your "who" confused with your "do." Your

true value

is found when you fully understand who you are in Christ.

"Therefore, there is now no condemnation for those who are in Christ Jesus, because through Christ Jesus the law of the Spirit who gives life has set you free from the law of sin and death."

ROMANS 8:1-2 NIV

You can be as cl
want to be. You ju
willing to put the
relationship witl

e to God as you
have to be
me into your
Him to get there.

"Come near to God and he will come near to you...." **JAMES 4:8 NIV**

You can be bitter or better. Let God use the hard things in your life to make you better!

"Consider it nothing but joy, my brothers and sisters, whenever you fall into various trials. Be assured that the testing of your faith [through experience] produces endurance [leading to spiritual maturity, and inner peace]. And let endurance have its perfect result and do a thorough work, so that you may be perfect and completely developed [in your faith], lacking in nothing."

JAMES 1:2-4

191

Prayer changes more than things – prayer changes you!

"Pray, therefore, like this: Our Father Who is in heaven, hallowed (kept holy) be Your name. Your kingdom come, Your will be done on earth as it is in heaven."

MATTHEW 6:9-10 AMPC

"For I want you to know, believers, that the gospel which was preached by me is not man's gospel [it is not a human invention, patterned after any human concept]. For indeed I did not receive it from man, nor was I taught it, but I received it through a [direct] revelation of Jesus Christ."

GALATIANS 1:11-12

We don't need more information; we need revelation.

"Blessed are the meek, for they shall inherit the earth."

—**MATTHEW 5:5 NKJV**

Meekness is not weakness,
it's strength under control.

"Be on guard; stand firm in your faith [in God, respecting His precepts and keeping your doctrine sound]. Act like [mature] men and be courageous; be strong."

1 CORINTHIANS 16:13

God has given us
an antidote for fear:
FAITH. When fear
knocks on your door,
send faith to answer.

It's easy to give people what they deserve; it's a privilege to give them grace and mercy.

"Above all things have intense and unfailing love for one another, for love covers a multitude of sins [forgives and disregards the offenses of others]."

1 PETER 4:8 AMPC

"Fear not, for I am with you; be not dismayed,
for I am your God. I will strengthen you,
yes, I will help you, I will uphold you
with My righteous right hand."

ISAIAH 41:10 NKJV

Courage

is doing what you know you should do even though you feel afraid.

Do it afraid!

Joyce Meyer Ministries
PO Box 655
Fenton, MO 63026
joycemeyer.org

Printed in the United States of America
First Printing, 2017
ISBN: 978-1-942854-08-1